Simple Recipes For Your Organic Veg

Andrea Parker, Boxed Green Co.

Go Green, Live Green, Boxed Green

Introduction

I deliver organic vegetable and fruit boxes across Bolton and Bury. Enjoying seasonal produce is what Boxed Green is all about. My veg and fruit boxes will always be fresh and nutritious. I will use local UK farmers whenever possible and source from warmer climates when necessary, by boat, no air freight. I love being part of nature, especially on my own allotment space. It gives me great joy throughout the seasons, watching the busy bees and butterflies, autumnal leaves, and snowy winters. Boxed Green is based in a quaint pump house in Belmont, surrounded by nature which is perfect! My ambition has always been to have my own business. In 2020 I was unexpectedly made redundant from the aviation industry. There's never been a "right" time to start a business, but becoming unemployed gave me the motivation I needed to embark on my new venture-"Boxed Green" Now I have finally hung up my wings, I am ready for a new chapter... I believe that making a small change to buying organic veg and fruit will benefit people, animals, wildlife and the natural world. Anyone looking to make a change to eating more sustainably and ethically whether you are veggie, vegan, flexitarian or carnivorous is welcome to try my organic produce but ask me for a strawberry in

December… it's a no! It isn't possible by mother nature's standards!

Andrea Parker

Contents

Cauliflower Steaks

I love cauliflower as a plant-based main meal and the possibilities are endless! For a quick and easy option have you ever tried cauliflower steaks?

They are super easy and what spices you decide to use is up to you. I made an Asian-style cauliflower steak here, but you could try herbs, spicy and cayenne pepper, sumac or whatever you fancy.

Directions:

Simply wash the cauliflower, remove the leaves with a knife but keep the core intact. Slice the cauliflower into one-inch-thick pieces. Lay the pieces on parchment paper, running oil onto each side (I use rapeseed oil). Add a sprinkling of your spices – I used garam masala, curry powder, paprika, cumin powder and touch of cayenne pepper mixed in a dish – and sprinkle over each cauliflower slice.

Oven cook on the highest heat for 15-20 minutes until golden. Turn over half way through.

Fennel

I personally dislike liquorice, which is what fennel tastes like raw. Roasted though, it's a different matter... It takes away the strong aniseed taste! Any frond (green wispy bits) can be used as a garnish. They taste a bit like dill.

Directions:

A tray bake is an ideal way to cook them and it's easy and straightforward.

❧ Cut the stalks off the fennel.

❧ Quarter the fennel bulb.

❧ Lay in a toasting dish with cherry tomatoes and sprinkle some caraway seeds, salt and pepper.

❧ Cook in the oven on 160°C for one hour or until caramelised.

Another good option…

is following steps one and two to prepare the fennel, add red onion wedges, lemon wedges, salt/pepper and a drizzle of olive oil and roast. You could also add some tinned butter beans, a squeeze of lemon and sprinkle on parsley. Add these twenty minutes before the end of the cooking time. This version also makes a substantial veggie mains.

Kiwi Dressing

I love a kiwi dressing. I drizzle it on salads, add to sandwiches or stir through noodles packed with veg!

Directions:

I use this quick and easy recipe. To get the consistency of a dressing you can peel the kiwi then add to a Nutri-bullet, food processor, grinder or use a mandoline to get the smooth consistency.

1. Peel and whizz up four kiwis and add to a mixing bowl.

2. To the mixing bowl add ¼ of a finely diced onion, ½ a squeezed lemon juice, 3 tsp of maple syrup/agave, ¼ tsp salt and a grind of black pepper.

3. Add a mild oil to loosen the dressing and whisk.

Diced kiwi can be added to ice cube trays and frozen. They can be added to G&Ts or soft drinks.

Or eat whole!! The skin is edible! Eat like an apple or cut into rounds.

Courgette Pasta

I love this quick and tasty courgette pasta. With just a few ingredients needed it's just what we need on chilly night.

You will need:

☐Courgette (I used x1) but feel free to use two if needed.

☐ Linguine/spaghetti pasta.

☐ Lemon.

☐ Salt & pepper.

☐ Oil for cooking.

Directions:

First of all…

☐ Cook your linguine to pack instructions.

☐ Grate half of your courgette. Heat a frying pan with oil and fry your grated courgette until browned (approx. 5 mins) set aside on kitchen paper (this is our crispy garnish!)

☐ Cut the other half of the courgette into matchstick size pieces and fry for 4 mins.

☐ Put a splash of pasta water in with the courgette, add the pasta after draining.

☐ Squeeze 1 lemon and some zest into the pasta.

☐ Check seasoning.

☐ Serve up! With the crispy fried courgettes on top.

This dish would also be nice with a sprinkle of parmesan or ricotta cheese stirred through.

Leek and Lentil Pie

Perfect for a rainy day.

And why not include a savoy cabbage side dish or pickled red cabbage.

You will need:

- x1 large leek (veg box).
- x1 tin of green lentils (or dried lentils soaked for 2 hours).
- potatoes – peel, boil and mash with milk, salt, pepper.
- soy sauce/tamari.

Directions:

First of all, slice the leek and fry in a pan on a medium heat and season with a little salt, add a few splashes of soy sauce if the leek starts to colour too much. You want the leek to be softened. Drain the lentils and add them to the leeks. Cook for a few minutes. Check seasoning and add more soy sauce if needed. Transfer the mixture to a casserole dish and top with mash. You could add some grated cheese if you wanted. Bake in the oven at 200°C using the oven and grill option, or just bake until the mash has some colour in the oven without the grill option.

.

For the savoy cabbage side dish.

❧ Shred half the savoy cabbage in your veg box.

❧ x2 garlic cloves sliced (veg box).

❧ 1/2 teaspoon of caraway seeds (or nigella seeds or cumin seeds, fennel seeds-don't add all the options! just choose one☺).

❧ Oil for stir frying.

❧ Salt and pepper.

Steam/boil the cabbage for 3-4 minutes... Heat up the oil in a frying pan, add the seeds and garlic slices for 1 min, then add the seamed/boiled cabbage stir fry for a further 3 minutes until browned-season with salt and pepper. Serve on the side of the leek and lentil pie.

Lentilognese

For an autumnal evening I love nothing more than a plant-based lentilognese

The homemade garlic bread is an option, but why not! I have eaten this meal many times and it never disappoints.

You will need:

- 125g dried Puy lentils (or if you prefer a can of rinsed green lentils.)
- carrot x1, finely diced.
- garlic 3 cloves, crushed.
- green pepper x1 (deseeded and finely chopped).
- 1 large onion, finely chopped.
- 400g chopped tomatoes.
- 375g veg stock.
- 1tbsp light soy sauce.
- 2tsp of vegan yeast.
- 350g of dried pasta shells.

Directions:

1. In a lidded saucepan add the dried lentils and stock and cook for 25 minutes. Take off the heat and keep to one side (keep the stock they were cooking in too).

2. Spray a non-stick pan with low calorie cooking spray, add onion, carrot, garlic and pepper and cook for 8 minutes.

3. Add the chopped tomatoes, yeast, and light soy sauce and simmer for 15 minutes.

4. Cook the pasta to the cooking instructions and drain.

5. Add the pasta to the vegetables along with the cooked lentils.

6. Season to taste and add chopped parsley.

I occasionally add mushrooms ♧ for some texture.

Lunch Noodles

I don't know about you but I find it hard to be inspired by lunchtime options. Not that I ever get time to have a "lunch break" after starting a new business☺ But it is something I am working on. If you are a business owner, working from home or about to return to the office (or even flight crew you can get a jar of veggies through security ☺) this recipe for a homemade healthy pot noodle is a good one.

I really enjoyed my lunch today. I tweaked it here and there to my own preference more ginger, lime soy sauce etc.

You can pretty much use leafy salad type veggies from your veg box.

You will need:

❧ x1 nest of noodles (quick cook – I used plant based beetroot noodles).

❧ 3-4 spring onions, trimmed and finely sliced.

❧ 2 small carrot, peeled thinly sliced (I used a potato peeler to make ribbons!)

❧ 6 mangetout/or a few frozen peas.

❧ 1 leaf of a cabbage/pak choi, finely shredded.

❧ 1/2 tsp of grated ginger.

❧ 1/4 of a green/red chilli, finely chopped.

❧ 2 tsp of soy sauce.

❧ juice 1/2 lime.

❧ 1/2 garlic clove, grated.

❧ 1 tsp of vegetable bouillon powder, or 1/4 veg stock cube.

Directions:

Put all the ingredients in a masonry jar except for the lime and soy sauce. At lunch time pour over boiling water to just cover everything, pressing the ingredients down. Cover and leave 8-ten minutes, stirring once or twice, then add soy sauce and lime to taste... and enjoy!!

The options are endless. You could try it with a mushroom and rocket/spinach combo and trial a few spices such as curry powder, and dash of cayenne chilli.

Mushroom Soup

On a rainy and cold day I love homemade mushroom soup.

We have all different varieties of mushrooms making regular appearances in the veg boxes throughout the year including Portobello, shitake, oyster, chestnut and button mushrooms. ♣

You will need:

♠ 1 tbsp oil

♠ 1 onion (chopped)

♠ 1tsp crushed garlic

♠ 1 tsp of dried oregano and basil

♠ 800g mixed mushrooms

♠ 2 tbsp of soy sauce

♠ 400ml coconut milk

♠ Salt & pepper

Directions:
1. Add the oil to the pan and add the onion, oregano and basil and sauté.
2. Add the mushrooms and soy sauce. Pop a lid on and cook on a medium heat for 10minutes.
3. Remove the lid and continue to cook for a further 10mins (mushrooms release a lot of water this helps to cook some of the water off)
4. Add the coconut milk and cook for the last 10 minutes.
5. Add salt and pepper and a fresh herb garnish.

Pasta Fagioli (using borlotti beans in the veg box)

The borlotti beans are versatile and can be used in salads or as an Italian side dish or in a casserole. I am personally going to make this rich pasta Fagioli recipe from Naples as it reminds me of my travels to Sorrento. If you've never visited the Naples region of Sorrento, Positano and Pompeii, go and book a trip there now! But first we need to cook the borlotti beans which is a meditation and a labour of love but well worth it.

You will need:

Borlotti beans,

1 garlic clove,

2 bay leaves

And salt to taste

Directions:

Peel and crush the garlic clove and peel and finely chop the onion.

Heat the olive oil in a pot (medium/tall walls)

Add garlic and onion, and sauté a few minutes, until golden.

Remove garlic and add beans and 1/2 teaspoon of salt. Add passata and mix.

Add pasta and water and cook 10-15 minutes, or until pasta is cooked "al dente". Give it a mix every now and then to avoid pasta sticking to the bottom.

If needed, add a little water.

You can add chilli to the pasta – this is personal preference!

A lovely juicy filling dish and fresh borlotti beans over canned will give amazing flavour.

Pineapple Rice with Coconut-dusted Oyster Mushrooms

This plant-based dish comes with a warning that you will eat all the mushrooms yourself! They can be made with or without the pineapple rice and added to salads or noodles. This dish transports me back to the Caribbean where pineapples are smoked on the BBQ and the curried spices bring out a sweet and sour taste.

For coconut oyster mushroom you will need:

- 100 g of mushroom (any mushrooms work: shitake, oyster).

- 2 tbsp of desiccated coconut.

- 2 tbsp panko breadcrumbs.

- 1 tbsp of Dijon mustard.

- 2 ½ tbsp of water.

- 1 tsp of agave syrup.

- ½ tsp salt, pinch black pepper.

Directions:

1. Preheat the oven to 200°c (400 degrees)

2. Slice the shitake/oyster mushroom thinly.

3. Take 2 mixing bowls, in the first bowl add the desiccated coconut and panko bread crumbs.

4. In the second bowl, whisk together the Dijon mustard, water, agave, salt, and pepper.

5. Then, take one slice of mushroom, dip in the mustard mixture fully coating so the mushroom is fully coated. Then put the mushroom in the coconut mixture. Press the coconut mixture on to the mushroom and make sure it is fully covered.

6. Repeat with all the mushrooms and then add them to a baking sheet, drizzle with oil/spray low fat spray and bake in the oven for 15-20mins until they are brown and crispy.

Pineapple Rice

You will need:

3 cups of cooked basmati rice.

1 onion, chopped.

3 cloves of garlic, crushed.

1 tbsp soy sauce/tamari.

1 tbsp of oil.

1 tbsp curry powder.

2 carrots cut into thin strips.

½ red pepper cut into thin sticks.

1 cup of pineapple cut into chunks.

Coriander and spring onion garnish (optional).

Salt and pepper.

Directions:

Cook rice to pack instructions.

Sauté the onion until translucent.

Add the garlic, carrots, pepper and cook for 3 mins.

Stir through the curry powder and add the pineapple.

Salt and pepper to taste.

Serve in pineapple boats!

Rainbow Rolls

Rice paper rainbow rolls are a great healthy add on to your BBQ or served with noodles as main dish or super delicious lunch option.

Directions:

The rolls are easy to make and tasty ☺

❧ Slice any of your veggies into thin strips about 3 inches long e.g. cucumber, courgette, spring onion, red onion, salad turnips, lettuce leaves, carrots.

❧ You will also need rice paper wrappers approx. 8 or as many as you want to make and fresh mint.

❧ Once you have sliced up the veggies set aside.

❧ Fill a wide bowl with warm water. Soak 1 rice wrapper for 15-30 seconds until pliable. Put the wrapper on a chopping board.

❧ Arrange a few of the veggies, leafy greens and herbs starting with the lettuce leaves.

❧ Wrap like a burrito, folding the ends into the middle, then folding over from the centre. Tucking and rolling tightly. The first one is always rubbish looking! but you soon get the hang of it... Repeat until you have made as many as you like.

❧ Cut the rolls in half so you can admire your colourful pieces of art!

Now you need a dipping sauce of your choice or just soy sauce will work. I used this combination from my previous recipe of Asian slaw. It worked well. I find pouring a little dipping sauce in to roll itself is better than dipping it gives the rolls instant flavour.

Dipping sauce

Mix all the ingredients together and taste and tweak to your liking.

- 2 tbsp of soy sauce.

- 1 tbsp clear honey or agave or maple syrup.

- 1 garlic clove finally chopped.

- 1 tbsp of finely chopped ginger.

- 2 tbsp of white wine vinegar or rice wine vinegar.

- 2 tbsp of toasted sesame oil.

- 2 tbsp of olive oil.

- Squeeze of lime/lemon juice (optional).

Red Cabbage

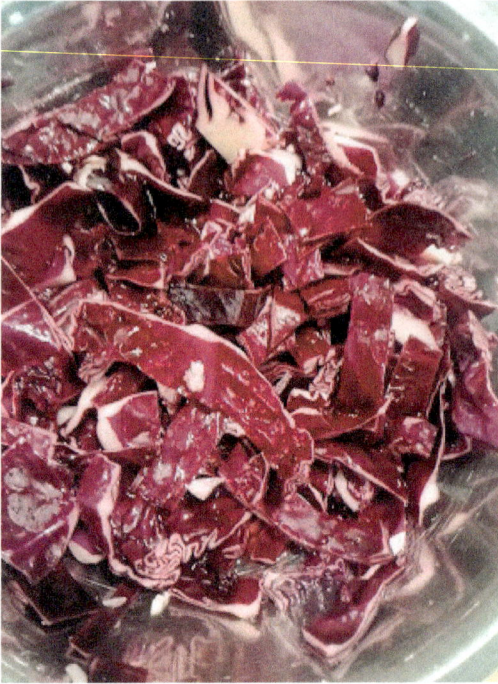

You will only need 1/4 of the red cabbage in your box to make pickled red cabbage. The rest can be used for tasty stir-fries and coleslaw.

This recipe is great, as it is ready in a matter of 2 hours, and keeps in the fridge in a bowl covered, for up to 2 weeks. Not that it will last that long!! Add it as a side dish to stews, turnip puff pastry pies or anything else you are cooking.

You will need:

- 1/4 red cabbage (veg box).

- 1/2 cup of red wine vinegar/apple cider vinegar – 120ml.

- x1 clove garlic (veg box) grated.

- 1tbsp sugar (I used agave it worked well too).

- 1/2 cup of water – 120ml.

- 1 tsp salt.

- 1/4 tsp ground black pepper.

Directions:

- Remove the core from the red cabbage, shred the cabbage with a knife.

- Toss the red cabbage with remaining ingredients and mix.

- Add to a sealed bowl/jar and store in the fridge for up to 2 weeks, but ready in 2 hours

Add to your burgers, wraps, stews... Enjoy!!

Slaw

This Asian-inspired slaw is super exotic and tasty. I had it with a salad and jacket spuds mashed with sautéed Portobello mushrooms also from your veg box.

You will need:

* 1 bunch of spring onions/red onion.

* 4 medium carrots, peeled.

* 1 small white cabbage.

For the dressing:

* 2 tbsp of soy sauce.

* 1 tbsp of clear honey.

* 1 garlic clove, finely chopped.

* 1 tbsp of finely chopped ginger.

* 2 tbsp of white wine vinegar or rice vinegar.

* 2 tbsp of toasted sesame oil.

* 2 tbsp olive oil.

Optional coriander roughly torn and lime juice.

Directions:

To make the Asian-inspired slaw simply...

☐Grate the carrot, chop the onions and shred the cabbage as finely as possible and add to a bowl.

☐For the dressing combine all the ingredients together and whisk. Make sure the honey has dissolved.

☐Pour the dressing over the veg and toss thoroughly. Leave for 10-20 minutes to soften.

☐ Serve the coleslaw with a sprinkle of coriander and a squeeze of lime juice (optional).

Sofrito Paella

If you fancy a break from the BBQ how about making a paella... I make my own sofrito (base of the paella) and I freeze it once cooled in 30g portions (per person) so I can just defrost and make a paella from scratch, even on a weeknight!

You will need:

- 400g tomatoes (veg box) (see method keep the skins for stock)
- 65g finely diced onion (veg box)
- 75g red pepper finely diced (veg box)
- 2 garlic cloves thinly sliced (veg box)
- 40ml olive oil
- 15 threads of saffron
- 15g chopped parsley.
- pinch of smoked paprika

Sofrito is the base of all paella. Stock can be homemade or shop bought. For a veg stock check out page 40.

Allow **30g** of sofrito **per person** (make sure you add enough). Add the sofrito to the pan and then add the paella rice **75g per person,** then add the stock **230g per person** season to taste**. Do not stir**. Keep the rice on a medium heat and cook for 20mins until you can hear the rice crackling. Check it is not sticking and put a tea towel/newspaper over the top for 5 mins.

Don't forget to add your protein into this recipe!! And cooking time. Serve with lemon wedges and parsley.

Directions:

- Use the big side of the grater, grate the tomatoes until you are just left with the tomato skin. (Keep the tomatoes skins to make stock).

- Heat your pan on a medium heat and add the olive oil. Add the finely chopped garlic, we want it to be a golden color as it brings out the nutty flavour.

- Add the 15 strands of saffron to the garlic and then add the chopped onions along with the chopped parsley. Cook this down for approx. 5 minutes.

- Now add the red pepper (sweat it out for a few more minutes and continue to stir the sauce to stop it from catching.)

- Turn the heat up and add the tomatoes to the pan as well as the smoked paprika and the salt. Cook for approx. 40 mins (at least).

- Run your spoon through the middle of the middle of the sofrito. If there is no evidence of water and the consistency appears "jammy" it's done!

Sushi

I am always on the look-out for new ideas for lunch options that are easy to create. I have always wanted to make vegetable sushi.

You can include so many veggies in sushi including peppers, spinach, carrots, sauté mushroom, avocado, cucumber, sweet potato, aubergine, mango, beetroot and lots more.

You will need:

- 260g Sushi rice (short grain Japanese rice).
- nori sheets (seaweed).
- 60 mls rice vinegar.
- soy sauce.
- 1 tsp salt.
- 2 tbsp maple syrup.
- sesame seeds.
- vegetables of your choice 🔲🔲🔲🍅🔲

Directions:

◎ Rinse the sushi rice in cold water and cook to pack instructions.

◎ In a bowl combine rice vinegar, salt and maple syrup.

◎ Add the rice to the bowl and combine.

◎ Place a nori sheet shiny side down on a bamboo rolling mat.

◎ Add a handful of rice to the middle of the nori sheet and spread it out, leave a 3/4 inch gap at the top of the nori sheet.

◎ Add strips of vegetables of your choice.

◎ Roll... I would recommend watching a rolling sushi technique video which is easier. I managed to make triangles, circles and squares!

◎ Slice up the sushi and serve sprinkled with sesame seeds and dip in soy sauce.

◎ Eat the same day.

Sweet Potato and Quinoa Chilli

This an easy one-pot chilli that has plenty of protein, essential fibre, vitamins and minerals. The quinoa adds a nice twist. I find myself making this dish often over the winter season.

You will need:

- 1 tbsp olive oil
- 1 medium onion, diced (veg box)
- 5 cloves of garlic, minced
- Spices: 1.5 tbsp of chilli powder, 1 tbsp cumin, 1 tsp dried oregano, a few dashes of garlic and onion powder
- Salt to taste
- 1 can of kidney beans, 1 can of black beans (you can use whatever beans you prefer: borlotti, cannellini etc.)

Directions:

- In a large saucepan heat the oil and add the onions and cook for 5-6mins until soft and the edges are browned.
- Add the chili powder, cumin, oregano, minced garlic, garlic & onion powder, quinoa, beans, diced tomato, sweet potato and broth/water stir to combine.
- Bring to a boil, reduce the heat, cover slightly (ajar) and cook for 30-40 minutes, stirring occasionally.
- Add more water to your liking and enjoy!

Turnip Puff Pastry Parcels

Turnip puff pastry parcels/saucers!

Turnips can be stored at room temp, they will last a lot longer in the fridge. They are varied sizes, I used just the largest of the two turnips (x1) in the picture to make 6 puff pastry saucers.

You will need:

❦ x1/2 turnips depending on size (veg box).

❦ puff pastry-I used fresh Jus-rol ready rolled puff pastry sheet. It's suitable for veggies and vegans.

❦ salt & pepper.

❦ red onion (veg box) <u>or</u> leek if you have any left from a previous week's veg box.

Directions:

❧ Grate the turnip, I blotted some of the moisture with a kitchen towel as the turnip mixture is quite wet.

❧ Fry off the onion/Leek, and then add the grated turnip and heat through.

❧ Season with salt and pepper.

❧ Meanwhile cut out the puff pastry circles approx. 5-7cm (I used the top of a champagne glass ☐)

❧ Spoon some of the turnip mixture into the middle of each circle, place another circle on top and seal the edges with a fork.

❧ Bake in the oven on 200°C until golden approx. 10 minutes.

Turnips like paprika, garlic, thyme and apple.

I found 3 parcels, steamed veg and a good helping of the homemade red cabbage (on another page) was a satisfying meal for a veggie.

Ultimate Plant-based Burger

This recipe was made with children in mind. As a veggie I have been through a lot of home-made veggie burgers!! But these are my favourite by far. I recommend them for anyone! They are great as you can pop them in the fridge (already cooked) and just reheat in the oven. These quantities made approx. eight big burgers.

You will need:

- 350g of potatoes (washed, skin on).
- 150g red onion, finely chopped.
- 150g small leek, finely chopped.
- 150g carrot, grated.
- 100g of mushrooms, diced.
- 1 garlic clove, crushed.
- 1 tsp fresh thyme leaves (optional).
- 1 tbsp soy sauce.
- 40g (vegan) cheese, grated.
- 75g of fresh breadcrumbs.
- 2 tsp of maple syrup.
- 2/3 aquafaba (chickpea water).

- salt and pepper.
- oil for frying.
- flour for dusting.

Looks an exhausting list, I know, but the top ingredients are sometimes in your veg box and the burgers will be worth it☺

Directions:

♨Prick the potatoes and microwave for 10mins or boil in a pan of water for 30mins. Set aside to cool.

♨ Heat the oil in a large frying pan and sauté the onion, leek, carrot, mushrooms, garlic and thyme (leave out thyme if you don't have any) sauté for approx. 10 minutes stirring occasionally until the vegetables are soft. The mixture should be quite dry and leave it to become cold.

♨ Peel the potatoes and lightly mash with a fork. Add the potato to the cold veggies along with everything else apart from the oil and flour (75g breadcrumbs, 3 tablespoons of chickpea water 2 maple syrup and 4g cheese, 1 tablespoon of soy sauce).

♨ Mix together and season well with salt and pepper.

♨ Shape into 8 burgers and chill in the fridge for 30mins.

♨ Lightly flour both sides, then fry in a little oil for about 3-4 minutes on each side until golden and cooked through.

They won't be around for long! However, you can keep them in the fridge for the next day or freeze them. I would recommend you cook them as above first... then wait to cool before individually wrapping them for the fridge/freezer. This is because potato sweats in the fridge if left un-cooked.

Simply take them out of the fridge/freezer and re-heat in the oven or frying pan.

Veg Stock

If you are stuck indoors why not make a vegetable stock to get ahead on the week. It can be refrigerated once cooled and also frozen. So whizz this up and add it your soups, risottos, stews. I fancy a veggie paella next week □

I generally use 3 medium carrots for stock but it depends on the size.

You will need:

☐carrots 2 large or 3 medium (veg box).

☐2 onions (veg box).

☐3-4 celery sticks (veg box previous if you have any left).

☐1 garlic clove (previous veg box).

☐1 tbsp of rapeseed oil.

☐1/2 a glass of white wine (optional).

☐a few peppercorns.

☐a sprig of thyme/a few parsley stalks if you have them.

☐1-2 bay leaves roughly torn.

Directions:

I like to grate the carrot, and slice the onion and celery finely. If you grate all the veg the stock only takes 10minutes. If it's been chopped 20-30mins is needed.

🌿 Heat the rapeseed oil in a large pan over a medium heat.

🌿 Add the vegetables, herbs, peppercorns, garlic (grated) and sauté for around 5 minutes, stir every now and then.

🌿 Add wine if using, then 1.75 litres of boiling water.

🌿 Bring to the boil then simmer for 10minutes if the veg is grated but 20-30mins if chopped.

🌿 Strain the stock and either use straight away, pop it in the fridge or freeze.

Stock is full of goodness! I find it great for meal planning, as I already have a paella, a mushroom and potato curry and a pepper soup on the agenda for this week all enhanced by veg stock.

A great way to spend a rainy weekend ☂

Notes

_____

_____

_____

_____

_____

_____

_____

_____

_____

_____

_____

_____

_____

If you have loved creating and enjoying my recipes I would love to see. Tag me into your social media posts/ send me your photos of your creations. Instagram/FB @boxedgreenco

Printed in Dunstable, United Kingdom

63631707R00050